This Book Belongs to:

· ·

Book Wishlist

Book Wishlist

TITLE		PRICE	BOUGHT
AUTHOR			

TITLE		PRICE	BOUGHT
AUTHOR			

TITLE		PRICE	BOUGHT
AUTHOR			

TITLE		PRICE	BOUGHT
AUTHOR			

TITLE		PRICE	BOUGHT
AUTHOR			

TITLE		PRICE	BOUGHT
AUTHOR			

Notes

Book Wishlist

TITLE		PRICE	BOUGHT
AUTHOR			
TITLE		PRICE	BOUGHT
AUTHOR			
TITLE		PRICE	BOUGHT
AUTHOR			
TITLE		PRICE	BOUGHT
AUTHOR			
TITLE		PRICE	BOUGHT
AUTHOR			
TITLE		PRICE	BOUGHT
AUTHOR			

Notes

Book Wishlist

TITLE	PRICE	BOUGHT
AUTHOR		
TITLE	PRICE	BOUGHT
AUTHOR		
TITLE	PRICE	BOUGHT
AUTHOR		
TITLE	PRICE	BOUGHT
AUTHOR		
TITLE	PRICE	BOUGHT
AUTHOR		
TITLE	PRICE	BOUGHT
AUTHOR		

Notes

Book Wishlist

TITLE		PRICE	BOUGHT
AUTHOR			
TITLE		PRICE	BOUGHT
AUTHOR			
TITLE		PRICE	BOUGHT
AUTHOR			
TITLE		PRICE	BOUGHT
AUTHOR			
TITLE		PRICE	BOUGHT
AUTHOR			
TITLE		PRICE	BOUGHT
AUTHOR			

Notes

Book Wishlist

TITLE		PRICE	BOUGHT
AUTHOR			
TITLE		PRICE	BOUGHT
AUTHOR			
TITLE		PRICE	BOUGHT
AUTHOR			
TITLE		PRICE	BOUGHT
AUTHOR			
TITLE		PRICE	BOUGHT
AUTHOR			
TITLE		PRICE	BOUGHT
AUTHOR			

Notes

Reading Log

Reading Log

TITLE		DATE	PAGE

Reading Log

TITLE		DATE	PAGE

Reading Log

TITLE	DATE	PAGE

Reading Log

TITLE		DATE	PAGE

Reading Log

TITLE	DATE	PAGE

TITLE	DATE	PAGE

Reading Log

TITLE		DATE	PAGE

Book Review

Book Title ______________________

Author ______________________   **Nationality** ______________________

Genre ______________________   **Year** __________   **Pages** __________

Memorable Quote	Page Number

Characters

Plot Summary

Notes

Rating

Book Title

Author

Nationality

Genre

Year

Pages

Memorable Quote	Page Number

Characters

Plot Summary

Notes

Rating

☆ ☆ ☆ ☆ ☆

Book Title

Author

Nationality

Genre

Year

Pages

Memorable Quote

Page Number

Characters

Plot Summary

Notes

Rating

Book Title

Author   **Nationality**

Genre   **Year**   **Pages**

Memorable Quote	Page Number

Characters

Plot Summary

Notes

Rating

☆☆☆☆☆

Book Title

Author

Nationality

Genre

Year

Pages

Memorable Quote

Memorable Quote	Page Number

Characters

Plot Summary

Notes

Rating

☆ ☆ ☆ ☆ ☆

Book Title

Author   **Nationality**

Genre   **Year**   **Pages**

Memorable Quote	Page Number

Characters

Plot Summary

Notes

Rating

☆ ☆ ☆ ☆ ☆

Book Title

Author   **Nationality**

Genre   **Year**   **Pages**

Memorable Quote | Page Number

Characters

Plot Summary

Notes

Rating

Book Title

Author

Nationality

Genre

Year

Pages

Memorable Quote

Page Number

Characters

Plot Summary

Notes

Rating

☆☆☆☆☆

Book Title

Author   Nationality

Genre   Year   Pages

Memorable Quote	Page Number

Characters

Plot Summary

Notes

Rating

☆ ☆ ☆ ☆ ☆

Book Title

Author

Nationality

Genre

Year

Pages

Memorable Quote

Page Number

Characters

Plot Summary

Notes

Rating

☆ ☆ ☆ ☆ ☆

book

Book Title

Author

Nationality

Genre

Year

Pages

Memorable Quote

Page Number

Characters

Plot Summary

Notes

Rating
☆ ☆ ☆ ☆ ☆

Book Title

Author   **Nationality**

Genre   **Year**   **Pages**

Memorable Quote	Page Number

Characters

Plot Summary

Notes

Rating
☆☆☆☆☆

Book Title

Author **Nationality**

Genre **Year** **Pages**

Memorable Quote	Page Number

Characters

Plot Summary

Notes

Rating

☆☆☆☆☆

Book Title

Author

Nationality

Genre

Year

Pages

Memorable Quote

Page Number

Characters

Plot Summary

Notes

Rating

☆ ☆ ☆ ☆ ☆

Book Title

Author   **Nationality**

Genre   **Year**   **Pages**

Memorable Quote	Page Number

Characters

Plot Summary

Notes

Rating

Book Title

Author

Nationality

Genre

Year

Pages

Memorable Quote

Page Number

Characters

Plot Summary

Notes

Rating

☆ ☆ ☆ ☆ ☆

Book Title

Author   **Nationality**

Genre   **Year**   **Pages**

Memorable Quote   **Page Number**

Characters

Plot Summary

Notes

Rating
☆☆☆☆☆

Book Title

Author **Nationality**

Genre **Year** **Pages**

Memorable Quote	Page Number

Characters

Plot Summary

Notes

Rating

☆ ☆ ☆ ☆ ☆

Book Title

Author   Nationality

Genre   Year   Pages

Memorable Quote	Page Number

Characters

Plot Summary

Notes

Rating

Book Title

Author   **Nationality**

Genre   **Year**   **Pages**

Memorable Quote   **Page Number**

Characters

Plot Summary

Notes

Rating

☆☆☆☆☆

Book Title

Author   **Nationality**

Genre   **Year**   **Pages**

Memorable Quote	Page Number

Characters

Plot Summary

Notes

Rating

Book Title

Author

Nationality

Genre

Year

Pages

Memorable Quote	Page Number

Characters

Plot Summary

Notes

Rating

☆☆☆☆☆

Book Title

Author

Nationality

Genre

Year

Pages

Memorable Quote

Page Number

Characters

Plot Summary

Notes

Rating

Book Title

Author

Nationality

Genre

Year

Pages

Memorable Quote

Page Number

Characters

Plot Summary

Notes

Rating

☆ ☆ ☆ ☆ ☆

Book Title

Author **Nationality**

Genre **Year** **Pages**

Memorable Quote	Page Number

Characters

Plot Summary

Notes

Rating

Book Title

Author   **Nationality**

Genre   **Year**   **Pages**

Memorable Quote   **Page Number**

Characters

Plot Summary

Notes

Rating

Book Title

Author

Nationality

Genre

Year

Pages

Memorable Quote	Page Number

Characters

Plot Summary

Notes

Rating

☆☆☆☆☆

Book Title

Author

Nationality

Genre

Year

Pages

Memorable Quote

Page Number

Characters

Plot Summary

Notes

Rating

☆☆☆☆☆

Book Title

Author   Nationality

Genre   Year   Pages

Memorable Quote	Page Number

Characters

Plot Summary

Notes

Rating

☆ ☆ ☆ ☆ ☆

Book Title

Author   **Nationality**

Genre   **Year**   **Pages**

Memorable Quote   **Page Number**

Characters

Plot Summary

Notes

Rating
☆☆☆☆☆

Book Title ______________________________

Author ______________________   **Nationality** ______________________

Genre ______________   **Year** ____________   **Pages** ____________

Memorable Quote	Page Number

Characters

Plot Summary

Notes

Rating

Book Title

Author   **Nationality**

Genre   **Year**   **Pages**

Memorable Quote   **Page Number**

Characters

Plot Summary

Notes

Rating
☆☆☆☆☆

Book Title

Author

Nationality

Genre

Year

Pages

Memorable Quote

Page Number

Characters

Plot Summary

Notes

Rating

Book Title

Author

Nationality

Genre

Year

Pages

Memorable Quote

Memorable Quote	Page Number

Characters

Plot Summary

Notes

Rating

☆ ☆ ☆ ☆ ☆

Book Title

Author   Nationality

Genre   Year   Pages

Memorable Quote	Page Number

Characters

Plot Summary

Notes

Rating

☆☆☆☆☆

Book Title

Author   **Nationality**

Genre   **Year**   **Pages**

Memorable Quote   **Page Number**

Characters

Plot Summary

Notes

Rating

☆ ☆ ☆ ☆ ☆

Book Title

Author   **Nationality**

Genre   **Year**   **Pages**

Memorable Quote	Page Number

Characters

Plot Summary

Notes

Rating
☆☆☆☆☆

Book Title

Author

Nationality

Genre

Year

Pages

Memorable Quote

Page Number

Characters

Plot Summary

Notes

Rating

☆ ☆ ☆ ☆ ☆

Book Title

Author   **Nationality**

Genre   **Year**   **Pages**

Memorable Quote	Page Number

Characters

Plot Summary

Notes

Rating

☆☆☆☆☆

Book Title

Author

Nationality

Genre

Year

Pages

Memorable Quote

Page Number

Characters

Plot Summary

Notes

Rating

☆☆☆☆☆

Book Title

Author ____________________ Nationality ____________________

Genre ____________________ Year ____________________ Pages ____________________

Memorable Quote	Page Number

Characters

Plot Summary

Notes

Rating

☆ ☆ ☆ ☆ ☆

Book Title

Author

Nationality

Genre

Year

Pages

Memorable Quote

Page Number

Characters

Plot Summary

Notes

Rating

☆ ☆ ☆ ☆ ☆

Book Title _______________________

Author _______________________   **Nationality** _______________________

Genre _______________   **Year** _______________   **Pages** _______________

Memorable Quote	Page Number

Characters

Plot Summary

Notes

Rating

Book Title

Author **Nationality**

Genre **Year** **Pages**

Memorable Quote	Page Number

Characters

Plot Summary

Notes

Rating

☆☆☆☆☆

Book Title

Author .... **Nationality** ....

Genre .... **Year** .... **Pages** ....

Memorable Quote	Page Number

Characters

Plot Summary

Notes

Rating

Book Title

Author

Nationality

Genre

Year

Pages

Memorable Quote	Page Number

Characters

Plot Summary

Notes

Rating

☆☆☆☆☆

![book illustration]

Book Title ....

Author .... **Nationality** ....

Genre .... **Year** .... **Pages** ....

Memorable Quote	Page Number

Characters

Plot Summary

Notes

Rating

☆ ☆ ☆ ☆ ☆

Book Title

Author   **Nationality**

Genre   **Year**   **Pages**

Memorable Quote   **Page Number**

Characters

Plot Summary

Notes

Rating
☆ ☆ ☆ ☆ ☆

Book Title

Author   Nationality

Genre   Year   Pages

Memorable Quote	Page Number

Characters

Plot Summary

Notes

Rating

☆ ☆ ☆ ☆ ☆

Book Title

Author

Nationality

Genre

Year

Pages

Memorable Quote

Page Number

Characters

Plot Summary

Notes

Rating

☆☆☆☆☆

Book Title

Author

Nationality

Genre

Year

Pages

Memorable Quote

Page Number

Characters

Plot Summary

Notes

Rating

Book Title

Author

Nationality

Genre

Year

Pages

Memorable Quote	Page Number

Characters

Plot Summary

Notes

Rating

☆ ☆ ☆ ☆ ☆

Book Title

Author **Nationality**

Genre **Year** **Pages**

Memorable Quote	Page Number

Characters

Plot Summary

Notes

Rating

Book Title

Author **Nationality**

Genre **Year** **Pages**

Memorable Quote **Page Number**

Characters

Plot Summary

Notes

Rating

☆☆☆☆☆

Book Title

Author   Nationality

Genre   Year   Pages

Memorable Quote	Page Number

Characters

Plot Summary

Notes

Rating

Book Title

Author   **Nationality**

Genre   **Year**   **Pages**

Memorable Quote   **Page Number**

Characters

Plot Summary

Notes

Rating
☆☆☆☆☆

Book Title

Author   **Nationality**

Genre   **Year**   **Pages**

Memorable Quote	Page Number

Characters

Plot Summary

Notes

Rating

☆☆☆☆☆

Book Title

Author   Nationality

Genre   Year   Pages

Memorable Quote	Page Number

Characters

Plot Summary

Notes

Rating

☆ ☆ ☆ ☆ ☆

Book Title

Author   Nationality

Genre   Year   Pages

Memorable Quote	Page Number

Characters

Plot Summary

Notes

Rating

☆☆☆☆☆

Book Title

Author

Nationality

Genre

Year

Pages

Memorable Quote	Page Number

Characters

Plot Summary

Notes

Rating

☆ ☆ ☆ ☆ ☆

Book Title

Author **Nationality**

Genre **Year** **Pages**

Memorable Quote	Page Number

Characters

Plot Summary

Notes

Rating

Book Title

Author

Nationality

Genre

Year

Pages

Memorable Quote	Page Number

Characters

Plot Summary

Notes

Rating

☆☆☆☆☆

Book Title

Author   **Nationality**

Genre   **Year**   **Pages**

Memorable Quote	Page Number

Characters

Plot Summary

Notes

Rating

☆ ☆ ☆ ☆ ☆

Book Title

Author

Nationality

Genre

Year

Pages

Memorable Quote | Page Number

Characters

Plot Summary

Notes

Rating

☆ ☆ ☆ ☆ ☆

Book Title

Author **Nationality**

Genre **Year** **Pages**

Memorable Quote **Page Number**

Characters

Plot Summary

Notes

Rating

☆ ☆ ☆ ☆ ☆

Book Title

Author | **Nationality**

Genre | **Year** | **Pages**

Memorable Quote	Page Number

Characters

Plot Summary

Notes

Rating

Book Title

Author   **Nationality**

Genre   **Year**   **Pages**

Memorable Quote	Page Number

Characters

Plot Summary

Notes

Rating

Book Title

Author   **Nationality**

Genre   **Year**   **Pages**

Memorable Quote	Page Number

Characters

Plot Summary

Notes

Rating
☆ ☆ ☆ ☆ ☆

Book Title

Author   Nationality

Genre   Year   Pages

Memorable Quote	Page Number

Characters

Plot Summary

Notes

Rating

Book Title

Author

Nationality

Genre

Year

Pages

Memorable Quote

Page Number

Characters

Plot Summary

Notes

Rating

☆ ☆ ☆ ☆ ☆

Book Title

Author   **Nationality**

Genre   **Year**   **Pages**

Memorable Quote	**Page Number**

Characters

Plot Summary

Notes

Rating

☆☆☆☆☆

Book Title

Author   Nationality

Genre   Year   Pages

Memorable Quote | **Page Number**

Characters

Plot Summary

Notes

Rating
☆ ☆ ☆ ☆ ☆

Book Title

Author

Nationality

Genre

Year

Pages

Memorable Quote

Page Number

Characters

Plot Summary

Notes

Rating

Book Title

Author __________________ **Nationality** __________________

Genre __________________ **Year** __________ **Pages** __________

Memorable Quote	Page Number

Characters

Plot Summary

Notes

Rating

☆ ☆ ☆ ☆ ☆

Book Title

Author　　　　　　　　　　　**Nationality**

Genre　　　　　　　　　　**Year**　　　　　　　**Pages**

Memorable Quote	Page Number

Characters

Plot Summary

Notes

Rating

Book Title

Author Nationality

Genre Year Pages

Memorable Quote	Page Number

Characters

Plot Summary

Notes

Rating

Book Title

Author

Nationality

Genre

Year

Pages

Memorable Quote	Page Number

Characters

Plot Summary

Notes

Rating
☆☆☆☆☆

Book Title

Author

Nationality

Genre

Year

Pages

Memorable Quote

Page Number

Characters

Plot Summary

Notes

Rating
☆ ☆ ☆ ☆ ☆

Book Title

Author   Nationality

Genre   Year   Pages

Memorable Quote	Page Number

Characters

Plot Summary

Notes

Rating

Book Title

Author   **Nationality**

Genre   **Year**   **Pages**

Memorable Quote

Memorable Quote	Page Number

Characters

Plot Summary

Notes

Rating

☆☆☆☆☆

Favorite Quotes

Favorite Quotes

TITLE

QUOTE

TITLE

QUOTE

TITLE

QUOTE

TITLE

QUOTE

TITLE

QUOTE

Favorite Quotes

TITLE

QUOTE

TITLE

QUOTE

TITLE

QUOTE

TITLE

QUOTE

TITLE

QUOTE

Favorite Quotes

TITLE

QUOTE

TITLE

QUOTE

TITLE

QUOTE

TITLE

QUOTE

TITLE

QUOTE

Favorite Quotes

TITLE

QUOTE

TITLE

QUOTE

TITLE

QUOTE

TITLE

QUOTE

TITLE

QUOTE

Favorite Quotes

TITLE

QUOTE

TITLE

QUOTE

TITLE

QUOTE

TITLE

QUOTE

TITLE

QUOTE

Books To Buy

Books To Buy

TITLE	
TITLE	
TITLE	
TITLE	
TITLE	
TITLE	
TITLE	
TITLE	
TITLE	
TITLE	
TITLE	
TITLE	
TITLE	

Notes

Books To Buy

TITLE

TITLE

TITLE

TITLE

TITLE

TITLE

TITLE

TITLE

TITLE

TITLE

TITLE

TITLE

Notes

Books To Buy

TITLE

TITLE

TITLE

TITLE

TITLE

TITLE

TITLE

TITLE

TITLE

TITLE

TITLE

TITLE

TITLE

Notes

Books To Buy

TITLE

TITLE

TITLE

TITLE

TITLE

TITLE

TITLE

TITLE

TITLE

TITLE

TITLE

TITLE

Notes

Books To Buy

TITLE

TITLE

TITLE

TITLE

TITLE

TITLE

TITLE

TITLE

TITLE

TITLE

TITLE

TITLE

Notes

Books Club Contact

Books Club Contact

NAME

PHONE

EMAIL

NAME

PHONE

EMAIL

NAME

PHONE

EMAIL

NAME

PHONE

EMAIL

NAME

PHONE

EMAIL

Books Club Contact

NAME

PHONE

EMAIL

NAME

PHONE

EMAIL

NAME

PHONE

EMAIL

NAME

PHONE

EMAIL

NAME

PHONE

EMAIL

Copyrights 2023 - All rights reserved